The Contracted World

Pitt Poetry Series

Ed Ochester, Editor

The Contracted World

NEW & MORE

SELECTED POEMS

Peter Meinke

University of Pittsburgh Press

The publication of this book is supported by a
grant from the Pennsylvania Council on the Arts

Published by the University of Pittsburgh Press, Pittsburgh, Pa., 15260

Manufactured in the United States of America

Printed on acid-free paper

10 9 8 7 6 5 4 3 2 1

ISBN 0-8229-5918-6

for *Herb, Aya, Wei, and of course Sophie Kathleen, for expanding our contracting world.*

Contents

Fish Tale

Poetry like anchovies adds a certain tang to life

more than most will bargain for
though we'll eat it in a pinch

Poetry won't yield an inch from its dark pallet in the store
naked as a scaling-knife
sharper than a bullshark's teeth

Fishshit pigshit bullshit sell sprightly in the magazines
crusting every page we touch

Lies like mullet spawned in hell graze the poisoned marketplace
sucking up each honest wish
soiling us from crest to crotch

With its cold iconic face camouflaged among the reeds
only poetry comes clean:

unpolluted angelfish

I

Left-Winged Sonnets

Brief Meditations on a Woodcut
by Leonard Baskin

The one who never looks up, whose eyes are lidded
And balled, like Blake's . . .
from Sylvia Plath's "Death & Co."

I
We must be careful whom we choose
for inspiration   or the muse
may turn upon us like an alien
that eats its victims from within

II
. . . eyes rolling inward see
round curve of skull the egg

the blank dome   screen
with the nerves in pattern

like razorcuts over the bones
of those who yearned to be good

but never understood
their mothers husbands wives

whose lives boiling in loneliness
burned and sputtered against the wall

where the innocent and cruel line up
before the state's wrath   the dogs of love

the invisible worm   the mad
blind muse of Sylvia Plath . . .

III
Happy poems are hardest because
you come off like a dog wagging its tail
instead of a worried soul who reads
the papers and inhales the flaws:
the brutalization of the frail

3

starvation and pustulant disease
nature still red in tooth and claw
whipping us daily   *How weary, stale,*
flat and unprofitable are these
hours days and years we stare across

And yet should we therefore fail
to see the young so very pleased
to be themselves?   I say Praise without pause
a damaged world deserving our applause

The Graybeards

O see the graybeards lip-synch sacred songs
to the true gods who rule unruly earth
enforcing laws of messianic games

divided up in sides where rites and wrongs
are neatly balanced   though No-one weighs their worth:

So how can we wonder why the world's in flames
when every faith implies an infidel
and every heaven sends someone straight to hell?

Marine Forecast

We wallow through the world white whales
in nature's gift shop thrashing tails
with jaws agape and stare surprised
when others curse our little eyes
that roll on either side but won't
see tentacles that lurk in front

and only Neptune who rules us all
cares that our hearts are large and full

Once haunted Ahab hunted us
for sins that ground his heart to dust
and those who hate like him will soon
be hoist upon their own harpoons
Though we can't predict how justice fares
we see our fate as linked to theirs:
Bound together sinking down
to where all whales and sailors drown

The Purity of Absolute Perfection

The purity of absolute perfection

has brought us to the Crescent and the Cross
by siphoning the blood of martyred saints
selling their bones like pretzels in the streets
And the *certainty* of faiths in their selection
works like a god's placebo: it takes the loss
of common sense for granted painting
painless heavens on tainted winding-sheets

Now they've woven rich embroidered tapestries
of Magi stars minarets and virgins
and thrown them over everybody's head
which wouldn't be so terrible if only
it would profit someone else besides the merchants

and didn't leave so many children dead

The Death of Friends

for W. S.

There are those who don't believe in death
It's natural they say   God's way
recycling the universe: The breath
of jasmine *our* breath   the jagged cries of jays
our cry   This golden rain tree petal
floats slanting to our table here
because the ashes of our loved ones settle
deep into the DNA of everywhere

This seems both hopeful and scientific
which is to say American: I'm sick
of it   Be logical until your brain turns blue
But he
will never come back   Nor she

Nor I nor you

Turkish Coffee

for Hamdija

Each time I fill the *jezve* I can see
and even smell the narrow lane and small
bazaar in Sarajevo where the three
of us sat cross-legged bargaining until
the set was ours   That was 1981:
we all held hands and swore the world was good
despite the rifles splintering the sun
along the mosques and churches of your neighborhood

More than coffee's turned bitter in this wreck
but I won't forget the charity in your eye
while you taught us patiently just how to make
it boil your English accented and sly:
*Remember to not fill your cup too full
and for best result: Go to Istanbul*

Elderly, She Paints Another Nude

The mirror has teeth: even my tongue feels
   wrinkled and skin that once was banned
in Boston hangs dry and spotty as these rags
I use to clean my brushes   O muse of Park-
inson's whose shaky hells advance like Meals
   on Wheels upon all fronts steady my hand
for one more work before the mirror cracks
   and all these clamoring images go dark

There's room in ancient heads for dreams of youth
   of either sex   bright eyes and satin skin:
      impossible to let these phantoms rest!
They weave behind weak eyes that can't in truth
      read the directions on my aspirin
   but see with mnemonic clarity your breast

The Director

for JRC

I can't write a cheerful poem for this melancholy Swede
who introduced us to uncertainty and existential
angst the absurd and the deconstructed   I can see him still
leaning through our doorway in 1961 with Jim Beam
and foreign names held out as burnt offerings magic seeds
for a parched garden so our heads uplifted like daffodils
in April as he said *Beckett Weill Brecht Frisch Pirandello:*
We didn't know we wanted them but Jim recognized our need

He was suspicious of tradition unless it showed
its bones so I confess up front that this is a sonnet built
of fifteen-syllable lines all declaring *Art's a bother*
we've got to bother with: our lives depend on it This truth flowed
like a northern river from his heart to ours with love and guilt

Old actor old bachelor dear old friend: Jim: you're our father

91st Birthday

for Kathleen Lewis

. . . so she sits mute on the long blue couch
knowing something important's happening
and these shadows around her   two women crouched
at her side one man at her feet are her offspring
(she's almost certain) who are talking
talking about *her* while notes flit and flare
in her head like firesparks and she wants to walk
away from them all toward silence anywhere

but the photos on her piano prove
when she was eighteen in 1925
her touch must have shaken every room
she entered showing there's a brief time bright
for everyone: a flushed spell when our blood comes
together the music all trumpets and drums . . .

Mystery

... so there's the fire escape   And too many keys

Beside the bed the empty glass accuses
no one   everyone   The Matron's eyes protrude
like gooseberries her glance startled when she sees
the Inspector staring at her knees

A page is missing from the book the Student
loaned the crippled Nurse and beneath the huge
black oak the Butler scrabbles in the leaves

Now gathered in the library the crime
gaping before us like a hungry hearse
we clear our throat we smooth our suit and dress

and now the Inspector turns for the last time
toward the Matron the Student the Butler the Nurse:

We stiffen like corpses crazy to confess ...

Caterpillar Plague, 2000

Inching toward us these creatures out of Poe

hump along our walks and walls like dreams

of someone terrified by worms all slow

and silent till you slip on one and scream:

disgust multiplied by multitude   Even birds

intuiting their taste won't risk a bite

Thus unimpeded and unsepulchered

they rise like hairy fingers in the night

Malacosoma disstria: Gorging pillagers

whose shit sifts down on us like mist or fog

they smear our village and all villagers

who venture out near oak or elm   What god

sharpened her nails and cut from what foul cloth

these larval lives ending in death or moth?

The Skiers

... time never disappears: the lost past
is never lost   i stand here on this mound
of time with you because my father asked
which way was west because his father found
the sea a way of life because his father met
in hannover a buxom peasant girl
because her farmer father tried to get
a wagon in the city
                    down

                        we

                            whirl
        the docketing hill   all slanted on
            our narrow sloping trace
        chains of lowercase letters gone
    before we reach what seems like space

when poles from frozen hands are flung:
pens for stories in a broken tongue ...

Treasure Island

Along the beaches sand lies blank as snow
on Christmas evening   Dying stars
fade in the foreign sky While children know
or guess they know what lies ahead: guitars
and games   white boxes and red ribbons
we wonder what this Christmas day will bring:
Not likely that our sins will be forgiven
not likely that we'll hear the angels sing

Nor was there snow in Bethlehem that night
but sand like snow shifted beneath the bright
star guiding kings across the desert drifts

So goes the tale and even if they crossed
in someone's dream and then got lost
we have our children still and we have gifts

Maples and Orange Trees, 2003

celebrating the twin birthdays of the
two St. Petersburgs, their 300th and our 100th

Our warm beaches and plump orange trees aren't the same
    as Russian lakes or ancient maples shaking in the winds
    that chill your city   In truth we've only had our names
    in common and now these birthdays too neatly pinned
    and labeled like sororal twins born centuries apart

        And yet it seems right to celebrate together
    Pushkin who loved parties would approve: Let's start
    a grand tradition with vodka and mimosas whether
    it's logical or not! Cities are built by dreams
and the broken hands of men and women by blood and tragic
    history serfs and Seminoles stoic hope that redeems
    despair transforming swamp and rubble into pulsing magic

For what are our two cities now if not sweet sites unfurled
    like sanguine banners signing for a better world?

Rocking Horse Winner

Leaning low in the saddle spurs scraping
the straining ribs of Silver peerless steed
in mad pursuit of murderers escaping
you gallop toward another noble deed:
Come on Silver! With every stride you gain
You spot the villains fire from a crouch
and hear with satisfaction groans of pain
as your dad rolls (reluctant) off the couch

With manly swagger you dismount fearless
and roll your victim over with your toe
then once again on Silver (peerless
steed!) rock into the western sunset glow

And I dying watch you fade from sight
packing toy pistols toward the coming night

Butterfly Cage

Something rings sympathetic strings
as flocks of mating monarchs fly
south on iridescent wings
to settle on our columbine
We're tempted both my wife and I
to warn them of the boy who springs
triumphantly with net held high:

But one can overdo these things

His captives seem to us like pages
torn from a picture book that's filled
with fading formal images:
to sigh for kings and queens in cages
that we ourselves have helped to build
is only natural as one ages

The Triumph of Desert Storm

. . . out of the blue horses'
steam rose like strings
as if they had been lowered into morning
by a great puppeteer leaning
above scrub pine and cedar
on my uncle's farm near Ocala

O and those horses towered
above me like battleships even at a distance
and my young eyes bore me bareback
soaring over Florida sand
below the white sun breasting
toward us through moss and mist

And below me the country
unrolled in a sweet pure
patchwork of abstract art
green and brown and yellow around
the still sparkling stars
of my father's cities . . .

Well this is the way to begin a poem
fairly easily tapping in
to the unconscious and leaping toward some
unrhymed memory or random invention
while even as we dream the homeless stir
beneath the *Times* on Central Avenue
morning kicking toward them like an officer
with notched nightstick and thick boots
The papers already brittle torn spotted
crackle and crow: *100,000 Iraqis*
slaughtered! spitting on proportion truth
a generation ruined and rotting
in the Gaza of our inner cities
and the tall blue horses of our youth

II
The Chemical Chain

The Contracted World

February when leaves sift down
like phosphorous
behind a sparking comet's dying thrust
above the cloudy gardens of our town:
azalea season   Puffs of pink
and white illuminate the shade
of limbs that twist out fifty feet and link
Brobdingnagian branches where handmade
children's tree homes hover: abandoned stations
above already fading constellations

Nearby a smokestack spits its bit
of sulfur on
the breeze affirming flowers will be gone
but pollution stays: nothing sticks like shit
Leaves for example: How they toil
not though on their descent they spin
adding rich acid to the sandy soil
decomposing even as Solomon
did helping to shape death's hypnotic wick:
part of nature's wisdom or nature's trick

Our vision's Lilliputian
Like falling rain
there's always one hundred percent of pain
available but its distribution's
random if not perverse   In San
Francisco de Nentón the troops
descended like a plague of dogs and ran
merciless from hut to hut   Here soft loops
of Spanish moss slip from the oaks   They tangle
in the blooms   That's what *we* see: that's *our* angle

How much of happiness should be
earned?   How much joy
in every accidental breath alloys

our just thoughts and natural sympathy
until we can't connect with lives
unfairly far away in all
respects? Next door our neighbor's seven hives
buzz like engines as he bends behind his veil
The end result: azalea–scented honey
It takes time   It takes love   And it takes money

P-town, '04

The word *free* curdles
in this expensive air
where gays and tourists
read the Sunday *Times*
and Bloody Marys cost
nine bucks a pop

Outside the café windows
a steady buzz of bees
disturbs the hollyhocks
doubling the faint vibration
of headlines naming bodies
in a war that costs us nothing

our major bother mainly
how to pronounce
Fallujah   Aljazeera
Ghazi Ajil   Abu Ghraib
So . . . we should be happy . . .
and yet there's still that buzz . . .

How to find peace again?
Let's try the official way:
Let's attach electric wires
to the naked legs of bees
and make them tell us *now*
where all the honey's gone

What Wild-Eyed Murderer

We shouldn't worship suffering: the world's
a spinning rack where suffering indicates
all goes well we're alive and not curled
up in the black hushhush death dictates
as its first condition: no screaming there

We crown ourselves with thorns of past
transgressions   Sharp spears of deed spare
no rib of pain: around the cross crashed
common lightning usual blood Who earns
our reverence should break both cross and crutch
in the face of suffering: while the rack turns

and tightens they'll smile at the sense of touch
Suffering's too common to be worth
anything   joy too rare to be priced
The saints we search for will embrace the earth:
what wild-eyed murderer suffers less than Christ?

The Deserted Village, 2002

Even the best villages are deserted
by someone their abandoned windows staring
like lonely women who have done everything
right all they were taught to do yet find themselves
at the end of life curled below a dark hill
with night drifting in and the cry of a barred
owl the single sound predicting the future

Sweet smiling village, loveliest of the lawn
now pale and hollow as a toothless yawn

Our mother played the piano and lovers
strolling by would pause peer into the cool room
where a young woman seemed lost in Debussy
and think that this was how life is meant to be
in a small town where you could walk anywhere
even away which is where our father walked:
Oh she'd have strangled him given half a chance!

Ill fares the land, to hastening ills a prey
where couples wake each day with less to say

I would bike to school up the steep hill around
the grand Hasken house where Mrs H had shot
the Chairman of the Board of Education
by accident (*Like hell* our father whispered
before he left fearing perhaps that Mother
would get ideas) the school composed of large stones
and small bones jelled in adolescent aspic

But now the sounds of population fail,
except around the mall or in the jail

Like a moth to its flame I often circle
by our empty house stop and get out my heart
that scarred philanderer jumping like a kid
again Today a fat spider sat spinning

her CD between our telephone wire
and laundry line and her song told me plainly
everything I loved was foolish and dying

The varnished clock that clicked behind the door
still ticks to me from time's diminished shore

Certainly we meant well like the citizens
of every town Pristina Columbine
Kabul Who doesn't want the good life with friends
at table the children safe music swelling
the air around us? Yet blades bloom in our hands
natural as daisies: the world addicted
to metal fitted for flesh like key to lock

But times are altered; trade's unfeeling train
shoots up our veins like moral Novocain

We have a photo of our parents Father
on his back arms perpendicular Mother
doing a handstand on *his* hands the godly
strength and trust of that Olympian moment
all we can ask of life Anything more like
a happy ending perhaps seems ... piggish Still
to see her dazed eyes today: unbearable

In all my griefs—and God has given my share—
the worst is this: that hope creates despair

Driving this morning I saw three men smoking
on top of a building-in-progress tiny
and soft against the iron beams The town is
dying streets yawn yet offices still sprout like
weeds with only people 'downsized' beauty gouged:
the pledged horn of plenty cheapened and betrayed
Triumphant parking lots cough through oily mouths

O Mother Father underneath the wave
we only wished for worlds beyond the grave

Inheritance

I seem to have inherited the wrong
things from my father: a fondness
for simple rhyme a thirst for strong
drink a tendency to get fat

Above all a certain meanness
of spirit an inability to forgive
or forget even minor transgres-
sions: I'll get him for that

The Spindled World

... the world is spindled on two poles
that hold in balance hot & cold
and rough & smooth   but now we're told
that scientists are filing down
the rough spots found in nature herself
and poets prophets red barbarians
will soon give way to blue machines
that neatly classify our genes
till even god is pigeonholed

by artificial seminarians ...

and now I see how birds on wires
punch out the sky unfolded above
like some huge card by IBM
about to fall on chicken little
and mother goose the whole damnation
unless some big black ugly crow
caw caw calling across the keys
breaks up the line with his harsh cries
of joy & woe and mutilation ...

The True UFO Story

Here's what they say: *I was abducted*
at two a.m. by small creatures
with huge eyes who inserted hairlike
probes into my brain . . .

Well why not? These are honest people
hordes of them! And yet we doubt   No one
likes to be conned and what are these times
if not one long disgraceful scam?   And now

against my will I have been chosen
to explain given this dubious gift
this Cassandran vision   Listen:
this is the true story

An unmarked star probing for eons
eastward like a Siberian tiger
beyond the cold Plutonian wastes of time
has come around to us   Its languid citizens

feed entirely on brain cells vast fields
of brain shuddering in their yellow air
like Greek sponges under water   This crop
delicate as the anemone needs constant

weeding pruning grafting of new life
new brainbuds on the ancient stock or else
it withers from repetition flushing
stale images through collapsing chambers

the language of loyalty oaths
and insurance policies bloating
the cerebra like ads for light beer staining
its cavities with darkling liver spots

For millennia uncounted they've raided
planet and satellite till only the dregs

of intelligence remain namely: us   This
is how they do it: a detector

pure selenium scans the earth searching
for original thought   On their screen
our world's a Sahara blank and bland
as a dean   But here and there pinpricks

of purple pick up a living brain and
they zero in   They know existence is
electric: matter mind and dream all
the idea of God at different frequencies

and God itself is variable modulating
from deities of weasels mice and corn
to Cronus Maya Shango They zero in
brushing every pulse the ox the falcon

and the poor patient oyster where it sleeps
within its pearly house   There are no 'little men':
only projections injected on our nerves
like silkscreen anesthesia while they perform

long-distance biopsy visiting our beds
the way Selene flew to Endymion each night
Painlessly they take their little samples
leaving these scooplike scars and we are left

a little more foolish than before while they
retreat in shadow like titanic forms
carrying our finest thoughts to reanimate
their brainfields   Their victims rub their eyes

and try to tell their stories: *I was floating*
over trees naked and unafraid We laugh
uneasily and unbelieving as Zeus laughed
when Pluto stole Persephone forever

The Simplest Animals

The simplest animals live in water
our natural solvent toward which we turn
like turtles toward the sea: mother & daughter
father & son yearn to be born again
seeking this dark baptism as primal truth

The human story is this search to recapture
lost youth through water   Our ancestor
the amoeba for example on growing old
simply splits down the middle & is young again
at once mother & daughter father & son

and the memory of this miraculous simplicity
is locked in the cells of our brain   When upon
some dry shore the first trembling pseudopod
stretched a tentative tentacle (which was
one supposes a gift from a starfish god)

we took our first step toward becoming wise
first step
toward good & evil house & plane:
then stomach nerves heart seed
and terrible brain

The Chemical Chain

Gulls

swooping in free-form arcs
above the sand
scoop up the same flat rock
over & over
thinking it's a clam

The most musical oriole
the drunkenest robin
have no choice but to make the standard nest

Only the human brain

dreaming the freedom of gulls & robins
can rattle the chemical chain
that binds the flow of our bones

while visions sweep like birds
trapped in a skull-like cave
wingtips brushing the walls
the night going mad with their cries
till a few of the strongest & luckiest

skip like stones from our eyes

The Little Factory, 1863

an early painting by Camille Pissarro

His women are walking
to the little factory   almost
a house under yellow clouds
telling us it's early morning

A thickened stillness fills the scene:
three women dressed in black approach
as if to church   One holds a child
The chimney's a steeple in the sky

matched by distant cypresses
on the right everything heavy
as God: this is ten years
before light shimmered from his brush

like the breath of thrushes before
he left and lost in Louveciennes a
thousand canvases fleeing
to London when the soldiers came

How he loved these women and
those clouds his life and theirs visible
in each thick stroke   The Germans
burned everything he left behind

And so when he returned and found
the paintings gone he set his easel
in the old familiar land-
scape at Pontoise: Began again

M. Hoffstetler's Last Class

a ballade set in a small school in Switzerland

Monsieur Hoffstetler brushed a tear
wrote his best English on the board:
School is a Pain in the Ass   Beer
is on me   This the *grande* reward
for our not jumping overboard
but sticking with him through his class
on grammar   *Nous étions* in accord:
Oui!   School *is* a pain in the ass

The tear was fake   but still it's clear
he liked us   Americans   bored
or *engagé*   were at least there
for fun   Who cared if we scored
like *les imbeciles* or never explored
his language   and couldn't pass
a seventh-grade exam   *d'accord?*
We: School is a pain in the ass!

Outside   the Alps glinted in sheer
blues and golds   and *les petits bateaux* moored
near the school bobbed bright with veneer
like the Swiss souls Monsieur deplored
when he drank his beer   *Mes pauvres   we hoard*
the Pompous Pills! he mourned   his glass
jealous toward the trim ships   *Ah   Lord*
oui . . .   l'école . . . pain . . . ass . . .

Monsieur Hoffstetler   we adored
you when you lay on the neat grass
scandalizing *le Directeur*   and roared
Wheee!   School ees Pain een the Ass!

Blackberry Jam

The mind reeks like a swamp
  another myth undone
  At least after reading Jung
we know we don't know what we want

Analysts nail us down
  on the flaming cross of desire:
  In a circus ringed with fire
my mind's a painted clown

Waving a cardboard knife
  I dive from a broken trapeze
  to land on shaking knees
and beg you to be my wife

Instead of stabbing your back
  I chew my raggedy nails
  Like a jar of blackberry jam
I hide my seeds in the black

The hell with them my love
  theories stink of the grave
  Let psychoanalysts rave
while we lie under the covers

Do I dream of an empty room?
  Does your Freudian half-slip show?
  We know we don't want what we know:
Carry me back to the womb

American Youth

What are American Boys Thinking About?
Sunday magazine headline

About a minute a day

the rest of the time they just horse around
And why not? What do American men
think about? We think about when
we were young horsing around with Betty

Stepanovich in Utica New York

What was American youth doing in Utica?
Learning to drink and smoke
to play the harmonica
to fix flat tires
Learning the jump shot
Learning to lie to Betty Stepanovich

Learning the difference between lie and lay

O let us drink but not too much
to the sweet lies and lays of our youth:
never our hearts so hot our hands so cold
frozen in front of the frightening beckoning doors . . .

How we despised the old!

Lilacs

With the fragrance of broken lilacs
the lost girls of our youth
haunt us like dead apostrophes

O my vine my christmas tree my
blue chip rainbow trout
where are you shining now?

My sunday morning heartbanger my
laughter benedictine my panic-picnic
are you still ringing today?

We cry crowded by images in an empty room
my root and branch my lost lilac
where do you live with whom?

On Teaching Our Son to Tell Time

Telling time is a complex business Peter
but there are some general rules
that we can follow: days
are longer than years sand
runs faster than tears
and nighttime hours are sweeter
No matter what they say we *are* Time's fools . . .

Time is circumference is hollow
the tube through which we hurtle
while the sun cools   Lives
run out like rabbits afternoons crawl
like turtles or like poets counting
coffee spoons . . .

and this small hand (yours)
covered by this large one (mine)
encloses rooms of time and love
my evening and your noon
while your hand pushes mine
to midnight much too soon

The minute hand is that large one
sweeping the moments before it like
crumbs from a crowded table
while the smaller one gathers the hours
an iron fist filled with flowers plucking
real blossoms real people leaving
the stalk of history a skeleton a fable:
Reaping reality sowing a mystery

Each little point is a minute not enough
time for a kiss if you learn to do this right
but time in it for murder or for cowardice:
time to burn The breath
of hate and fear pants quick in the mind's night

Watch out for the minute Peter: time enough
for many kinds of death

You tell time by taking the number
the short hand's accusing
(that's the hour you're losing) plus
five times the number the long
hand's brushing away (those are the minutes
you wasted today) The second hand's
optional up to the whim of the master
but steady as heartbeat Steadier: the heart
with certain hands beats faster

And that is *how* to tell time but
what to tell it is a different
thing Maybe you can look it
in the eye and say My dad taught me
to tell you: do your damnedest you'll
find me ready
Though you sink your scythe
in us up to the helve we will rise
together big hand little hand
at the stroke of twelve

Is that too dramatic? Then
just say I know you old man
old blusterer
and know what will make you yield:
I'll race around your meadows armed with love
and gather every flower from your field . . .

but this small hand (yours)
covered by this large one (mine)
encloses rooms of time and love
my evening and your noon
and your hand pushes mine
to midnight much too soon

The Wedding: February 26, 2000

In February in Florida all things seem possible:
spring lifts its arms and deer pick their delicate
way through thickening vines   Butterflies
on their instinctive journey rest upon open azaleas
closed tight up north   Double stars mated for life
like rare whooping cranes glide from east to west
through the clear skies of a new millennium
All of this partly mechanical: monarchs cranes
philodendron stars and deer all pulled
by gravity's attraction and the earth's

magnetic field along paths measured
and irregular: *these accidents were meant to be*

This morning the sun rose over the Bay
flattened like a wafer at the edges
partly obscured by smoke blowing from Bradenton
but up it came gilding the horizon
and the street where David and Megan
turn toward each other at the right moment
true as a compass the alchemy of their marriage
transmuting our ways and walks into a landscape
where every step is pulled in the right direction
each footprint dusted by weightless gold

The Timaya Tree

for Tim & Aya

Looking up
at the whispering tree
whose light blossoms drop
like *bon mots* at a garden party
we can see why the timaya
is known as our wittiest tree
Its rainbow petals decorate our hair
while deep roots delve East and West
as its branches lift musical arms
in a democratic circle embracing
weather of every sort and on gusty days
they sing back at the wind like mocking-birds
Every year in early September couples
gather beneath the tree to hear its song
and though of course it can never be truly translated
the lovers know in their hearts that these are the ones:
the words
they had
wanted to
whisper
all along

Epithalamion for Two Scientists

Einstein said *God doesn't play dice with the universe*
He was thinking of quantum theory but I'm thinking
of Peter and Wei starting ten thousand miles apart
beyond the East River and the East China Sea
light years of heaving mountains and multitudes
the golden chrysanthemums of Yunlin
and the purple violets of New Jersey
to join together this morning in May
in America on Long Island near Great South Bay

The uncertainty principle seems to tell us
everything's random   dice dreams and dragons
lightning and love   but not today:
This feels preordained   Some scholars claim
we don't *comprehend* theories but just
get used to them   So in the same way
we shouldn't try to understand poems
but only whisper them over&over as we will
to your children and your children's children like this:

Once upon a time Peter and Wei
were married one mild morning in early May
and all the violets and chrysanthemums
from Taipei to the waves of Great South Bay
danced like bright kites above their gardens
all because (Einstein and I would say)
Once upon a time
Peter&Wei
got perfectly married one certain morning in May

The Bookshelf

Lying flat on the floor because I'm old
and it's good for my back
counting coins of dust in the twilight
and squinting at the books huddled above me
like immigrants in ragged overcoats
guarding their family secrets
I think *You have cost me everything:*
stoopshouldered nearsighted soft and white
as a silverfish caught in the binding
of The Complete Works of Henry James
from hours days decades spent bent
over your pages when I could have been
pruning azaleas or hitting tennis balls with real people
Now I've been down so long

I'm too stiff to get up or even reach for a book

so I call for help not expecting an answer
but from the stern and shadowed shelves
Emma and Anna and all the lost inaccessible
women above me cry out with their special accents
words I understand only from their rhythm and inflection
O sorrow   they say all of them over and over
Carrie and Carol and Cora and Julia *sorrow o sorrow*   Catherine and Scarlet
and Sonja and Daisy *o sorrow sorrow*
Molly *o sorrow* Wendy *sorrow* Dora Maud Helen Hester
and I like any man who has blindly loved
understand too late as unhappy endings pour down
just sentences on their weeping and guilty prisoner
pinned to the floor by threads
of vanishing light

Song from the Wrong Bay

෨෩෪

Lights above Coquina Key
glow like Monte Carlo's or any diamond-crusted shore:
dollar signs across the sea

but it's only Tampa Bay
Big Bayou St. Petersburg where schools of skittish mullet surge:
mini-buffalo in May

On the Key accountants stroke
executives with peeling backs advising them to duck a tax
donate clothes to poorer folk

Our home's on the northern side
of Big Bayou We don't expect to greet the governor-elect
gliding on the evening tide

Nothing ever happens here
Dolphins rolling in a row parody a Disney show
We eye them and we pop a beer

toast the turning universe
Above us comets streaking toward Jupiter like a silver sword
litter a distracted earth

In the breeze from off the sea
velvet petals circle twice: agitated violet mice
beneath the jacaranda tree

If you stay here you'll be dead
brain eroding like the beach caving in at Pirate Reach
a dying friend of ours once said

She may be right   We've never met
Major Moguls out of Hell to teach us how to ring the bell
like Topsy on the Internet

A green heron near this oak
carved in stone against our sky stares at us with yellow eye
but doesn't move: familiar folk

we're harmless and *nothing* ever
happens here: Egyptian birds posture while we gum our words
dragging with the druggy weather

warm before and warmer after
smoothing out our nation's rage boiling on the paper's page
hearing only local laughter

It's not necessary to
believe in god or country when you perceive with common sense
this common sky's unblemished blue

the sun strobing off the sea
streets safe enough today although we all know or ought to know
tomorrow's rude catastrophe

When the citizenry think
we're only guilty if we're caught convicted in a court of law
our country's on its way to sink

like the sun in front of us
dropping bloodily below the brazen Gulf of Mexico
to circles cold and barbarous

From behind us comes a bark
bullfrogs summoning their mates sounds that turn the summer night's
romance into the brutal dark

Farther off a siren wails
Someone's done for someone says   Overcrowded hospital beds
spell the overcrowded jails

No one knows the antidote
Birds and bullfrogs aren't wise but most of them can recognize
there is some shit they will not eat

Recognition: Only this
can save us from the breaking wave pinned again inside a cave
insects in a chrysalis

a metamorphical reverse
shriveled monarchs curling back towards their viscous larval sac
doomed by some genetic curse

＊＊＊＊

Still   nothing ever happens
here   Ship-shaped   Coquina Key surrenders slowly to the sea
cargoing its pudgy captains

Planets gaze upon our scene
like tourists watching fiddler crabs along the beach perform their dance
primitive and Byzantine

Dear because I brought you here
in the bad old-fashioned way there are words I ought to say
before the last stars disappear

To clear its gills a mullet breaks
the surface like a rocket launch its scattered phosphorescent splash
bright as fireworks   It takes

just this to make us glad: our
joy lies in every detail danced before our eyes: this pale
beach those lights the jacaranda

and home behind us in their full
impermanence   There are those who say for happiness we close
our eyes   I open mine until

I see you here below the stars
(how many times beneath this tree?) petals staining you and me:
Coral messages from Mars

III

from *The Night Train & the Golden Bird*

1977

The Night Train

In its closed compartments
the fingers of suicides curl loving
around pens and knives
carving out on paper and skin
the poem of their lives
taking the night train to nowhere
rattling the tracks at 90 miles per hour
their futures unrolling behind them
each agony each cry repetitive
as railroad ties statistically boring

The train compartment is the perfect thing
better than the cancer clinic with
its pale green walls and plastic chairs
old copies of *Better Homes* and *True*
the opaque rippled glass showing also green
like the walls like patients chewing their lips
fingers twitching for forbidden cigarettes
better than the $6 motel room with
its two dim lamps and revolvable TV
the large mirror before the flimsy bed
the Gideon Bible the roaches in the bath
the people in these places already dead
their fingers drum the drumroll of their wake
on train compartment windows When they take
their lives it is the right place
this closed anonymous world inside a train
a nothing sort of place   For God's sake
get on with it: there's nothing much at stake

The Patient

Disease has expanded my horizons
and pain
spread the good word

Since I've been sick
I feel close to the blighted things of nature
(I myself am a blighted thing of nature)
     burnt oaks
     gutted houses
       (for surely houses are as natural as beehives)
     broken foxes lying by the highway

     bugs crawl along the rims of my glasses
     my body pocked with spiraled holes
      like those punched in butter
     in each hole something   moving

hooked on disease (it gives
meaning to my life) I wriggle wormlike
around the pain and God
is the large-mouthed bass circling
below me

Morocco

Marrakech Meknes Fez Casablanca
names on a map deep in our minds
Minarets & almond trees laying long shadows
cobblestone streets under keyhole arches
shine in the darkness like broken teeth

The soul is a camel
with a hump full of sentimental images
clumping across real deserts
seeking the perfect oasis that is no mirage
(no one has ever reached it)

Marrakech Meknes Fez Casablanca
the walled cities are truly beautiful
and corrupt   In the center they decay
like molars the pain is spreading
a white path for revolution

What shall happen to the almond trees?
They shall be burned with bazaar & babouche
their seeds shall burst underground from the heat
Green shoots will spring up
their bitter leaves nibbled by lost camels

The Great Wall

It would all be so simple
if only the waves would roll in smoothly
up to the great wall the children sit on
or the black rocks stay in their toothy row
or the laughing gulls with their hangmen's hoods
would neatly pick up the clamshells to drop on the rocks

but swollen with malice the waves reach ragged arms
for the children the rocks keep moving around
like giant crabs and the gulls keep picking up
rocks they think are clamshells
& dropping them on the rocks but they
always miss and pick up another & drop it
& miss with the terrifying patience of the insane

and there is always one child missing

Gramma

My grandmother was like your grandmother:

she hung in there played pinochle
and watched the Dodger games
until they took her to the hospital

and when I visited (home from school)
I embarrassed the family
by vomiting in the corridor
all those tubes in the nose in the arm
of Gramma who was tougher than I

And when she came home to die

after four days of not eating
asked for a half grapefruit and died
in Mother's arms   No one had seen her
get up but in the closet were folded
neatly her burial clothes

A little lady she demanded
little gave much and
enjoyed what was available

There's a lot to be said for hanging in there

Bones in an African Cave

Bones in an African cave
gave the show away:
they went violent to their grave
like us today

Skulls scattered on the ground
broke to the brain
The missing link is found
pointing to Cain

Children in the streets
pry up the cobblestones
Old instincts repeat
in slender bones

To our violent sons
beautiful and strong
caps in their polished guns
I hymn this song

Grow tall and free and wild
strong-voiced and loud
Be proud of the fierce blood
that won't die out

All things repeat
after the floods and flames:
new boys play in the streets
their ancient games

Neuchâtel Swans

dine wanly on pretzels
which they hold in their beaks
like firemen carrying children

Our children swim in cold green water
diving off stones below
the splayed feet of swans unafraid
of anything anything

They don't fear the blue shadow
turning circles deep in the water
there are no sharks in Lake Neuchâtel
but what the hell is that shadow?

They have heard of the black swan
who eats geraniums they have seen
the tall gates of the houses
close like beaks

but it's all a story
Scare me daddy tell me another story
And one day there he is son of a gun
there on the horizon sails the black swan

immense and satisfied white
geraniums in his mouth
preening toward the children who swim out

little pink fingers

Cheerios

You are what you eat & I
I am a sexmad wheatgerm
floating in holes of cheerios
stamped out of Kansas farmland
where in late August
the All–American sun
drives ripe farmgirls into barns
and shadows as pitchforks
are abandoned like Neptune's
trident while he rolled in the springs
with Ceres seeds exploding
everywhere pinecones and
pomegranates ears of corn
popeyed with heat
bunches of grapes swollen
in the wagon while we
danced & sang & drank
& ate and the god laughed
& chanted crying
Gobble it all in excess of
the minimum daily adult requirements:
screw hunger
look longer
live younger

Vegetables

'Just because they can't say anything
doesn't mean they don't hear you coming'

tomatoes in particular feel pain
thin girlish skin and
seeds quaking in jelly at the first prick
and carrots shrieking silent
like St. Bartholomew as you peel them
from foot to head: they feel

they feel   Disemboweled peas

slide into tumbrils dizzy
with air beets bleed on the
sinkboard celery wilts with its heart
in our hands squash
turns pale on our tables
and when you pick up the knife

and walk across the kitchen shoeheels softly drumming
even the coarse hydra-headed potato hears you humming

Poem to Old Friends Who Have Never Met

When I'm not wishing I could find a unicorn
I wish all our old friends knew each other
The very least they deserve
is the pleasure of each other's company

We'd go down by the river
and the rocks would hum
with this rich collection of men & women
They would look around and see themselves
no longer isolated

no longer points in the darkness pointing nowhere

but as links in a magnificent chain of
impossible flowers
girdling the world and their talk
(they are *all* talkers)
would burst like spray in the sunlight

and I would smile
saying nothing
with a bottle of beer in my hand
and a small white bird banging in my heart

Sunday at the Apple Market

Apple-smell everywhere!
Haralson McIntosh Fireside Rome
old ciderpresses weathering in the shed
old ladders tilting at empty branches
boxes and bins of apples by the cartload
yellow and green and red
piled crazy in the storehouse barn
miraculous profusion the crowd

around the tasting table laughing and rolling

the cool applechunks in their mouths
dogs barking at children in the appletrees
couples holding hands so many people
out in the country carrying bushels
and baskets and bags and boxes of apples
to their cars the smell of apples
making us for one Sunday afternoon free
and happy as people must have been meant to be

The Anchor

Father kept an anchor in the basement
huge and barnacled
an illuminated text for the children:
This house will stand   Old sailor
old soldier he steered through wars
and storming northern seas straight as a die
only to lose his course in suburban New York

Anchors are made of iron
and so was my father
and though I don't understand what makes things magnetic
so compasses spin like gyroscopes rolling downhill
and a man veers at an ankle or pales at an eye
he showed me love is varied as shells on a shore

and
though compass and anchor may guide you and hold you in port:
like the flare that illuminates trenches in the smoky night
like the disease whose rays brighten the fevered eye
like the bear whose roar brings the wilderness to its feet
romantic passion is the lodestar of this world

Angels Drink

for JOB

Everywhere
over the spinning world
cognac is evaporating
drifting unseen through the sober air
which accounts for the irregular motion of certain stars
and the high price of cognac

Gentlemen something must be done:
everyone to his station!

My project is a world–sized tarpaulin
sewn from the skins of aristocratic gerbils
raised entirely on muscadine seeds
All I need now is the zipper
I shall slip it on the world like a magic wineskin
and then

then ladeez & gennelmen
Life will be a Five-Star Holiday!

On Saturday nights I'll give an extra tug
and drops of cognac
will sprinkle the earth
like the tears of intoxicated angels

J Randall Randle

J Randall Randle was an undercover
poetry lover   On bottlegreen links
he'd knuckle the pockets of his narky
knickerbockers duck in the grove by
the 13th hole where he shanked
his Spalding   & pull out the wrinkled
lines on Prufrock thin & balding

On raindark evenings walking the dog
he'd snap down the brim of his tan fedora
snap up the collar of his London Fog
& tie the lout to a doctor's bumper
while he read by penlight in alleys
off murderous cobblestone streets
Down by the salley gardens
My love and I would meet . . .

One evening when he returned he found the thread
broken which he had taped over his fake bar and
knew that someone had turned around the false
bottles and seen his poetry books lined up
like bullets in a belt and 2 weeks later when
Billy Hines casually asked at a party Say Randy
what's a sonnet? J Randall Randle stalked him
home for 14 blocks and shot him iambically kaboom
kaboom between the lines

The Golden Bird

The mind can't sing a poem without the eye
that staring inward changes tree to Tree
with roots and branches in the inner sky

The world's a place where real birds really fly
into a distance only children see
The mind can't sing a poem without that eye

The birds disperse the stormclouds terrify
while children watch the wild electric tree
that roots and branches in their inner sky

The clouds disperse the children raise a cry
to see a rainbow curving toward the Tree
The mind can't sing a poem without that eye

The birds return the scattered children try
to find the gold that's buried near the Tree
that roots and branches in the inner sky

The clouds return   Children grow old and die
The Tree remains a golden bird nearby:
the mind can't sing a poem without the eye
whose roots and branches touch the inner sky

IV
from *The Rat Poems*

1978

At 1 a.m. the Moon Pops Out

God's tennis ball
This time
I'm ready for it
but the rats are ready too
They go back back
I'm amazed:
They use a two-handed backhand!

At 3 a.m. Music Begins

The rats are listening to Mozart & Schoenberg
I get up & sit on the stairs I like music too
They seem to prefer Schoenberg
At least they huddle near the speaker
where the strains of *Pierrot Lunaire* make
their delicate ears tremble like violins
I myself prefer Mozart
and would like to get closer to *that* speaker
But I'm afraid to move: rats
make me feel so
large

At 4 a.m. a Rat Crawls Over My Chest

I pick up the icepick

At 5 a.m. the Rats Rise

like the mist
like the people rising on all sides
like Mr. Sakeotis the butcher rising
through the clouds
shaking his gleaming cleaver
at the rattails
of the sun

At 6 a.m., Awake, I Think About Rats

No wonder   They're chewing my toenails
my fingernails

When we die our nails keep growing
so the rats have something to eat
Nature's way of showing
who's boss

At 7 a.m. I Look Closely
at my bed: crumbs & rat turds
in the folds of the sheet
the hair on my toes sticky
from the tongues of rats:
the examined life
is the pits

At 9 a.m. the Rats on Mars
walk gingerly around the Viking spacecraft
keeping behind the cameras as they turn
sniffing the iron legs nodding
their fine heads their bright eyes nodding and
smiling

At 11 a.m. I Collect Rat Quotes
My kingdom for a rat
My love is like a red red rat
A rat in time saves nine
There are rats in the belfry rats in the mold
rats in my sweetie's pants nine days old

At Noon the Rats Are Skateboarding
in the attic
They christie along the beams
One hot dog performs
a stacked nose wheelie   I
slip him some skin

At 2 p.m. I Write a Rat Haiku
Warm rain and wet wind
rat weather licks up the land:
the Devil's soft tongue

At 3 p.m. It's Snack Time for the Rats

I put out Sun-Maid Raisins
California Seedless
in a box
They eat the box too:
good eating anytime!

At 4 p.m. I Hold the Bleeding Rat

in a paper bag just pried from
the screaming hand of our son
who found him almost torn in half
by the neighbor's dog And still he bit
and still he fights scratching the bag
by my sweating leg as I race to the vet's
for tests So much life in that broken body
the bag thunders in the car the bag itself
cries Pain cries Blood cries
Murder!

At 6 p.m. the Enemies of Rats Conjoin

Owls skunks hawks they band together
coyotes weasels mongooses in cahoots
to stamp out rats But it can't be done
Medical science intervenes: it needs them
Everything we know about the ductless gland
is due to our friend the white rat

At 9 p.m. the Rats Are Making Love

in the missionary position
That is on
the missionary

At 11 p.m. the Blackest Rat of All

the plague rat the blood rat
settles in my dream its teeth locked
in my heart It's you I'm dreaming about
Sally Schwartz you & your red mouth
and small white teeth

At Midnight I Say My Prayers

Give us this day
our daily
rat

V

from Trying to Surprise God

1981

Trout

Struga Poetry Festival 1979

Look! how the bright green water spills
like dye from the spring to stain the darker
blue of Ohrid Lake   Muscular eels
weave in & out and the trout flicker

The magic Macedonian trout are under siege
their eggs devoured by California trout
larger but less tasty   One thinks
Capitalist swine!   General Motors!   CIA!
But no: California trout
were dumped in the lake by the Albanians
who never apologize never explain They wear
white skullcaps or black fezzes weave
in & out of the mountains like a secret code

Grape brandy peach brandy
juniper and plum
white coffee Turkish coffee
laced with rum

In the first-class hotel schools
of force-fed poets flicker and eddy
Ah the big poets eat the little poets
they nibble each other with tentative teeth
the little ones lurk in the shadow
of a large drink: *na zdrowie!   Skol!*
In the lobby poems pile up like peppers
dried out but dangerous get your red hots here!
I bite a fat sestina terrific!
In my heart the blood weaves in & out
half-alcohol by now whispering drunkenly
in the pool of my ear: *Trout* it hisses
remember the trout!

In the blue ring of mountains
as the sun climbs
the road weaves in & out
like hidden rhyme

Our driver is clearly insane and happy
doesn't speak English but likes to try
Fuck Stalin he says smiling passing
a horse and wagon on a blind curve
I keep my eyes on the road   I'd like
to be an *old* poet some day   Maybe tomorrow
By the road fields of faded sunflowers
nod like unread poets in the naked light
Behind them muezzins mount their holy missiles
pointed at Allah's eye: they too
on the hour chant and cry

Yaseen   Marit   Rafael   Klaus
Albert   Marianne   Tomasz   Staus

Why is it we always turn toward the small things?
The guide drones on about St. Sofie's Church:
The wide of the walls is seven meters . . .
Magnificent and yet you turn and say
See the bees in the rose tree see
that wreath of peppers on the wall!   Best of all
turning a corner we saw the old poet
standing alone beneath the dark-beamed homes
blue cap tilted weathered jacket
lost or lost in thought   His words weave in & out
of my mind starquakes in an inner galaxy
casting its cold and hopeless light
on an ocean of blood
The California trout *will* eat the Macedonian trout
We start things and they acquire
an energy of their own
until we're swept away at last and stand
like the old poet alone

in the alley of our bones
waiting for the end with fingers crossed
not exactly lost   I think my life has been spent
underwater   May God protect old poets
in their loneliness

Even here politics and passion
blossom like a sore
one is called a fascist
one is called a whore
Poetry knows no borders
its country is the soul
but where are the Russians?
the Bulgarians?   the Poles?

The trellised arbors the old tiled rooftops:
the men are dancing in the street!
How does that house keep standing?
And the Turks did this and that
in the Seventeenth Century or was it the Eleventh?
Why can't I remember these centuries?
This mosaic floor was Third I'm almost sure
but just as the guide explained
the disco band below the fortress blared

I pick a thorn from the rose tree
you pick a rose from the thorn tree
I pick a pear from the plum tree
you pick a plum from the pear tree

Among the dancers with linked arms
the old poet weaves in & out   Are you surprised?
he asks   No I am not though his poems
have surprised me for years
Pop-eyed poets prance in a circular fashion
slivovitz and coffee battle for control
And when I held hands with Yaseen
I was alarmed

by the warmth of his hands
The long Indian and the little Indian
make formal gestures   I bow you curtsy
I am seeing visions!   Ghostly silhouettes
of poets follow them on stage like
electric auras the old poet's almost
detached from him a dancing partner
a pure white mirror image   In our room
our arms weave in & out they
weave in & out
and suddenly I know that I am blessed!
We shall make love on the beach Macedonian style!
We shall drink cold white wine and swim to Albania!
We shall write a poem to the old poet and slip it
under his door   Yes   We won't wake him
We'll slip it under his door

God bless all poets small and great
God bless this fading tapestry
and bless the trout in Ohrid Lake
doomed in their darkness shining free

Letter from Warsaw, 1979

for Kathleen McDonald

Copernicus sits on the heart of Europe lost
in thought his back to the Academy
on the corner of Nowy Swiat the New World
His noble brow is dark his hand outstretched
the day itself is dark and cold the month
the year the boots the eyes the bones the ashes
In his left hand he holds the galaxy
in his right (sometimes) a pigeon also dark

The universe is dark ˙he says the sun is farther
than we thought
                    The mind is free

He swivels his huge head   He looks behind
You never heard this he says   Don't quote me
He shuts his blackened eyes   They open shrewdly
as I pass   Change money? the pigeon cries

Here as everywhere the couples interlock:
more so than Paris more than Rome because
the Poles are perfect existentialists
neither happy nor free   We burn like arrows
from the classic bow in helpless flight
or heat-led missiles nosing out the warmest
target to destroy on contact   The bleak
apartments bloom through smoke
a futuristic garden where paranoiac
petals blow in the northern wind
Mother to what shall we cling?   You'd say *Love*
and Music Both grow here: one trembles
without privacy in crowded buses
taverns thin-walled rooms   The other
an alcohol available to all
spreads its dark pool

to close our eyes and numb the abscessed pain
Surprised by tears I listen to my friend
with unpronounceable name playing the *Polonaise:*
even the chandeliers applaud flowers
enough to fill a common grave

What is art but God in the blood
crying to get out into this world?

Mother
I remember listening to you play Chopin
the *Marche funèbre* Sonata in B-flat Minor:
nothing too difficult or esoteric
your trembling fingers and panic-stricken eyes
in the dark house in Brooklyn where Grandpa
and poor paralyzed Uncle George refused
to talk to one another for thirteen years
Chopin then was a lesson to be learned
He still is In Warsaw they played his music
punishable by death in shadowed rooms
off old Krochmalna Street long since destroyed

Arts isn't democratic after all
it isn't equal: children
don't write the *Polonaise*
their prodigal fingers plunking out
virtuoso combinations without heart
The static music of computers
blossoms in patches of dry paralysis
like *Walden II* or rolfing or
illustrated manuals of sex:
they soil the air with blooms unholy
and irrelevant Mother you wanted beauty
for your children and fresh air Where
can we go but to the dignified cathedral
whose soaring arches stretch us beyond ourselves?

The first law is clarity or should be

82

to see   as under a microscope   what's killing us
the shape of evil   the number of its heads
the teeth in each head   the sharpness of each tooth
To taste its brass and filth   to make
the tongue retract   mouth dry up   the throat constrict
till every breath is pain   Clean to the bone
Then to begin again

The second law is beauty   or will be
when our cities are leveled to the ground
and the trees planted   When houses
go up there will be space between them
high ceilings   and relations between the spaces
where light and air mingle like music
on our souls   I told you once we had none
and you cried   But you were right:
I feel it here in Warsaw with the strains of Chopin
rising through the fog above the river
that has seen the beating heart of Europe
bleed like a crimson torrent down a slope
till every stone grew slick   And still the music sings

Ah   mother   you Irish romantic
you would love the Poles   You burned for beauty
in a world recalcitrant
to poor girls from Brooklyn   You did all your work
and more   Your teachers were as ignorant
as the fat pigeons burbling by our door

Mother   my brave darling
the third law might have been
Love your mother
But we have too many laws
so the third law is
There shall be only those two laws

Happy Hour

for Frank Dreisbach

Sweet alcohol god of afternoons
who carries in the crook of your elbow
the olive and the olive branch unsheathe
your plastic sword from the flaming stone
and pierce for us perception's swinging doors
En garde Monsieur Fear take that
and that Monsieur Ennui you rat
lie down with your mouse Regret

Let memory waltz with roses
and time disappear in the mist
Let the mirrors weep with happiness
at our pagan Eucharist

O there will be a great consummation
there will be a righting of wrongs!
If the telephone rings we'll ignore it
while we sing the sad old songs
We're not afraid of the telephone
or the dark with its grinning toad
we're not afraid of the night tonight:
let's have one more for the road
Common sense should tell us
we pay with pain for our sins
but we won't pay till tomorrow:
today everyone wins!

Common sense will tell you
drinks and love don't last
Waiter here's looking at you
Lover fill up the glass

A Necessary Bucket

Klunder men of sensibility
and moderation are outraged at your lack
of taste   Lying behind bulldozers
is messy and unheroic: it distresses
our practical nation which sells
vacuums and abhors waste
Your death proves nothing the fact
of your bones crushed in the April air
only proves what we've said all along:
crackpots and bright-eyed radicals
are always wrong making the wrong moves
for the wrong reasons We can't hurry
the seasons: the winter of our discontent
is with us until spring and so
if it doesn't break storefront windows
let freedom ring

Legislation and debate have proceeded
(at a stately pace) for a hundred years
from the emancipation proclamation
(which wasn't much of a start)
to the present in producing what's needed
to feed the dark beating
of the human heart While the efficient
silent typewriters recorded the compassionate
words making no sense at all
of efficient unsilent Southern senators
you nestled in the mud like the ground-
hugging plover (making no sense at all)
and got yourself run unromantically over

Was it suicide protest or accident?
Was your heart anguished at
the implacable world seeing all the lost
children all the love turned and twisted
laughter frozen and tears burned?

Or was your own life unhappy
a failure did you want it to stop
did you want to die sprawling in the mud
adding your insignificant drop
to the bucket of blood? Ah Klunder Klunder
in this inhuman age how could you make
such a sad and human blunder?

Was it suicide protest or accident?
Does it matter after all does it matter
to you or me?   Perhaps it's just this:
so much blood is necessary
to finally tip the scale
It doesn't matter how we fill
the pail and you
Presbyterian minister Bruce Klunder
lying broken in the mud
have added your drop to the necessary bucket
of black blood

Preacher, Said the General

Preacher said the General
are we not able
to carve a cane or a
stick for the glory of God?
Why art thou wroth? and why
is thy countenance fallen?

This rifle now, the M-1
I'm offering you isn't it beautifully balanced
(though obsolete)?   The curve
of burnished stock
fits snugly the shoulder socket
Is it not sweet to hear ka-rack
of the spinning bullet the downward swerve
of adjusted trajectory
zeroing in to the sheeplike target
SMACK at a mile away?
What do you say: isn't that
satisfactory?

And tell me isn't
a man-made cloud
a terrific thing?
(harder than fire and
softer than cumulonimbus
warmer than summer
and louder than birth and hot
with the holy desire
of man for dominion
over every thing that moveth
upon the earth)

And is this not
our burnt offering
mounting to God?
Are we not Abel

whose smoke rose
from bubbling flesh
to meat-eating heaven
driving the vegetarian Cain
east of Eden
to the land of Nod?

The Hunters: Southeast Africa

Stop! Four men are stalking through the underbrush
slipping like shadows shoulders close to ground
Their silent figures deepen the leafgreen hush:
the Headman the Hunter the Shaman and the Clown
They have killed Time these dark men who crouch
for weeks beneath the sub-Saharan sun
whose women dig for roots and weave a couch
of twigs and grass and cook with riverstones

And heart and mind and instinct work as one:
the Headman blazes through their spotted way
the Hunter kneels zeroed on their prey
the Shaman blesses the victim in its blood
and the Clown will tell the story when they're done:
the rules are clear as those before the Flood

Look! There are four chambers of the heart
on city street as well as tropic plain
and four directions where we all can start
and four dimensions and four kinds of pain:
tiger pain maggot pain elephant and shark
Four is the balanced number the four of spades
lies on the table accusing in the dark
We've marched on: only our blood has stayed

And of course we can't go back back to the bush
or desert back to the simple places where
soul and body fuse in the antique air
They weren't really simpler anyway
and yet ... something gave us a push
until we shattered like a pot of clay

Listen! Deep in the blue North the one wind blows
To the South a yellow flame flares in their eyes
Like a lantern in the West the red leaf glows
while a green star arcs through Eastern skies

Listen! I'm trying to be simple: four
men are stalking through the underbrush they
are in your blood you are a hunter or
you are the hunted and they're on their way

And we lie helpless as a broken wing
Seeking the secret of wholeness we are lost
in houses we have built at enormous cost
but tonight let's howl at the moon that matriarch
of all divided souls and we can sing
of tiger pain maggot pain elephant and shark

Greta Garbo Poem #41

When I'm with Greta Garbo
she gets very talkative
She likes me to put on my Russian accent
and she plays Ninotchka again
People think we're crazy
especially the waiters at Howard Johnson's
Do you want dessert? they ask
Oh no says Greta Garbo
Ve vant to be alone!
and she & I laugh and laugh and laugh

To an Athlete Turned Poet

Fifteen years ago and twenty
he'd crouch line-backer gang-tackler
steel stomach flexing for
contact contact cracking
through man after man   weekend hero
washing the cheers down
with unbought beer

and now his stomach's soft his books
press out his veins as he walks
and no one looks

but deep in his bone stadium
the roar of the crowd wells
as he shows them again
crossing line after line
with crackling fingers heart red-dogging
with rage and joy over the broken backs
of words   words   words

Threnody

for Ruth Clark

The box was brown the dress blue
the lips bright red: it wasn't you

There were certainly many flowers though
you never liked cut flowers We passed
the Gold-O-Rama yards crammed with junk
a car with a bleeding deer stuffed in the trunk
The chauffeur spoke of hunting quail: last
time out he got fourteen He dressed in red
from head to foot: a lot of nuts you know
go hunting these days He joked and said

This here hearse cost thirteen-five
you're lucky to get out alive

You would have liked that Your quiet heart
embraced so many people
The sun broke through clouds at the start
of the procession then perched on a steeple
near Route 46: that was hard to bear
But soon skies darkened: twenty-two
cars with lights on went slowly through
mist and traffic through the oppressive air

Harlequin trees in black and white
danced your welcome into night

Identical houses not unlike yours
watched from beyond the hill where you were hid
Rain sifted down Wind whispered across
the false grass And though I never did
I meant to tell you that in truth
you were named right though now you sleep past caring:
Ah Ruth Ruth
only the compassionate are daring

Miss Arbuckle

Miss Arbuckle taught seventh grade
She hid her lips against her teeth:
her bottom like the ace of spades
was guarded by the virgin queen

Miss Arbuckle wore thick-soled shoes
blue dresses with white polka dots
She followed and enforced the rules:
what she was paid to teach she taught

She said that Wordsworth liked the woods
that Blake had never seen a tiger
that Byron wasn't always good
but died in Greece a freedom fighter

She gave her students rigid tests
and when the school let out in June
she painted rings around her breasts
and danced by the light of the moon

Recipe

Let's say you want to write a poem
yes?
a good poem maybe not 'The Second Coming' but
your hair is getting thin already and
where's your 'Dover Beach'?

Everything seems somehow out of reach
no?
all of a sudden everyone's walk-
ing faster than you and
you catch yourself sometimes staring not at girls

You live in at least two worlds
yes?
one fuzzy one where you always push
the doors that say pull and
one clear cold one where you live alone

This is the one where your poem is
yes?
no
It's in the other one
tear your anthologies into small pieces
use them as mulch for your begonias and
begin with your hands

The Artist

He liked best watching TV
Next was shading all the maps
his father threw at him: *Maybe
you'll learn something despite the tube
You can color them in*
The felt-tipped pens from the studio:
wet black the deep blues
orange   yellow   kelly green

At first he followed the lines: France
was purple Australia blue all of Russia
a deep brown not red   But soon the colors spilled
over the lines and over each other: a mess
His father was a successful artist: *Successful
artists are stronger than their children otherwise
you kids gobble us up*
red orange yellow green blue black black black

He'd move through the spectrum warm and cool
darker and darker toward the center:
country   state   city   street   home
Nothing in this world blacker
than his room   Even his father couldn't find him here
Color is psychological his father said
Pink is the color of laughter
black white green yellow gray red red

When he turned off the TV
he would fall into that little white dot
and pop through the screen
to the nowhere where nobody lived

Intensity is what he was after

VI

from *Night Watch*
on the Chesapeake

1987

On the Bus in D.C., 1980

1920: the Russo-Polish War

In Warsaw no one had change: clerks
gave you matchboxes in its place
Because I was slow in counting
I walked the streets a human firework
terrified of some impetuous embrace:
You are American?   I love you! And up
we'd go a fireball disturbing the passersby
rushing to wait on lines   But in Washington
I save my quarters nickels feathery dimes:
I can hardly get on the bus my pants
are so heavy and my body chimes
like some metallic choir
as I sway in a flat-footed stance
longing for Warsaw and all those matchsticks
light as fire

Warsaw has always been on fire the Poles burn
with a dark internal blaze that blows their eyes
to madness Yet everything
stays somehow unconsumed: their cities flare
and crumble into ash conflicting winds
swirling across the plains carry the ash away
until it covers every inch of ground
from the Baltic to the twisted Dunajec
No soil is pure in Poland the ghetto
sprouts in cabbage and potato their apples
bitter with defeat   and
the dream-fed cities rise again
ringed by graveyards loved beyond belief
Where are the Jews of Poland?   Their ghosts
float everywhere their heavy-hooded eyes
swerve in the darkness searching for release

On All Souls' Night the penny candles
tremble the birches and the tulip trees

99

crosses stretch out endlessly the dates
so often young: 1925-1941   1929-1944 . . .
In the middle of the circle of the brightest light
thousands of candles lick the smoky air
ethereal witness to a passion still as stone:
a single obelisk thrusts a single date

In Washington we hold no sense of history or
history is something to be made maybe Wednesday
From the Capitol to the meanest house
the message flows: oranges
on street corners shoes
in windows polo players and
police on horseback   Everyone is healthy
even the muggers exercise daily
consume less fatty meats more fiber

but in Warsaw they know abundance dissipates
There are ghosts more permanent than buildings
Even *Stare Miasto* the Old Town is half
the age of our president Wherever two Poles meet
the spark jumps the dream connects
a building is begun: it moves
it grows it sways and breaks apart
and comes together somewhere else   I think
of this in Washington where everyone
seems incomplete: colliding atoms
particular discrete   while Poles are frozen
in a stream of energy that circles
on itself and lights itself and then explodes
or might explode Nobody knows I know
this is my stop my pockets bulge
I miss my matchsticks

The Pin

Perhaps their eyes flooded and closed because
our water earth and air are so impure
that only drowning with its blinding kiss
can clean us to the bone   The flesh sinks in
temptation and disease the mind winks
like a buoy in the night the needle
of the heart points always in where the child
squats sulky and unsatisfied like Ahab
in his cabin
                  Once in grade school
my parents and I were called
in frantic haste to see the X-rays shot
the day before: a pin hung near my heart
hard as a hook within that watery field
When had I swallowed it? What could be done?
I imagined I would die   Not till evening
did Mother recall the pin that held
my undershirt's torn strap
                    And still today
as we round Point-No-Point on Chesapeake Bay
jets ticking the waves like suicidal gulls
I feel that pin inside me where it never was:
mourning for lost poets in the pilot house
I move in spirit toward those sailing ships
across whose graceful bows the cold eye
of the radar goes blip blip blip throwing
their temporary image on the screen

Lordship Lane Station

a painting by Camille Pissarro

Aimed at the vague migrations of the clouds
the tall chimneys keep their secrets now
and the wounded houses sleep like exhausted guards
dreaming of captive birds their restless bones

Now the train coughs like a primitive message
its smoke thick and white as feathers or foam
flying or flooding and thinning and joining the sky
in a frenzy of loss and energy beyond all words

The train must be taking you somewhere
nearer your goal my daughter dark-eyed dove
leaving behind the holly the pitched roof
the black crucifix of the telegraph pole

Wherever you go this town will always be here
except for that patch you carry away in your blood
circling around and around in repetitive darkness
touching the underground stations your personal cross

Weeds

She planted marigolds because they kept
the bugs away   Their ridged bitter gold
glimmered like coins against the ivy and swept
brick of the walkways   She piled all the old
oak leaves from last fall around
the thick camellias with their waxy shine
In rows of alternating spice: silvermound
mugwort tansy basil sage parsley thyme
her garden spread outward from the center
an orderly progression from bergamot
to spearmint satisfactory and shared
But at the farthest point from where you enter
there in the oak's shadow in the central spot
she left some weeds untended where they flared:

stubborn ragged unassimilated wild

The Sheep

In the Alpine region a soft avalanche
whispered through space shoulder to shoulder
curling over the cliff soft furry boulders
bouncing from branch to bleeding branch

One thousand sheep in Bourg St. Maurice
lowered their heads their feet beating in unison
over their green pastures voices bleating
together sun red on white fleece

No reason given the pasturage was good
plenty of grass to eat water to drink
But the shepherd was gone they thought (if sheep think:
maybe they only listened to their blood)

Maybe they thought he never was coming back
but had gone off yodeling down
through the mountain pass forever   Alone
they could have been frightened by dogs or hawks

black dogs with rake teeth slavered
with hunger for meat hawks with talons
curving to hook into flesh: what's a gallon
of blood to a dog or a hawk? They wavered

huddled together on the mountain rise
They waited for a voice but no one spoke
and hearing the hawk's cry they hunched their shoulders and broke
pulling their own wool over their own soft eyes

A Dream of Third Base

for Sterling Watson

Night after night frozen at third base
I lean toward a throw I know I must catch
but don't stretch far enough:
the ball sails off the runner
slides snarling at my feet   Then
right away and once again
bare-handed as before the fall
perched on third in the starless air
the runner's shadow darkening the path
I wait for that accursèd ball

I think I'm afraid it will sting:
the ball is coming too fast
the catcher with his thick wrists
has reared and fired like a loaded gun

or the snake-eyed shortstop whose lidless eyes . . .

Surely baseball stands for something else:
I haven't been a fan
since the Dodgers abandoned Ebbets Field
We used to go on Sunday my dad and I
breaking the Fourth Commandment . . .

The field is Paradise then all green and new:
we're young and quick of foot our cries
fly in the springtime air

And then we're given a ball
And then we're given a bat
Who are those men in black?

It starts hurting after that

But why for me *that* place? '*Nel mezzo*
del cammin di nostra vita, I awoke on third base'

105

Dante would have loved baseball all those nines
and threes (even the stands stand
for something else: howling gluttons
stuff hot dogs down their throats)
I crouch at third the corner eternally hot
with Eros on the mound and Thanatos at bat
while the citizens stomp their feet
waving doleful undershirts
remembering the thick wrists of my father
the infield's skin the ball with its stitches turning
Drafted into this dream
by some archetypal team
my cleats dig into the dirt
my hand already burning:
guilty small and hurt

Sonnets for a Diabetic

I

Sentimentalist you loved words like *doom*
and felt it stalking you through foreign halls
but at the end they found you in your home
unromantic in that familiar room
alone forgetful: insulin withdrawal

In your back pocket some pills keys the comb
you seldom used and an unfinished poem:
you never finished poems Instead you'd call
late at night one by one your sleeping friends
reciting in that Appalachian drawl
your wonderful one-liners like a groom
wooing his bride with shining bits and ends
of jewelry before the night descends
My life you said *lies taut upon the loom*

II

In your rich brain the end must have burned better
even while crawling toward the phone you loved:
some images exotic from your trips
some grand betrayal some unanswered letter
had brought you to your knees in pools of blood
and you blew out with poetry on your lips

I hope so   Old friend to see you slip
away without a scene! Today I rubbed
my eyes and half expected you to rise
and look around pull on your thin gray gloves
stride out into our stricken winter weather
and waving at the birds to shout: *Surprise!*
But nothing happened   Again I rubbed my eyes:
I saw the last time that we drank together

III

We sat beneath the jacaranda tree
catching the purple petals in our beer
a royal carpet soft under our feet

That was *your* effect: anyone could see
this was just another dingy bar too near
the traffic to be comfortable the heat
not helped much by the scraggly tree and Pete
the bartender surly cheap and mean   Here
once more you spoke your lines   just last July!
It was your way of publishing: 'No mere
book that no one reads or needs but a free ·
voice to a friend who won't forget' And I
remember: *All day long the day goes by*
A lovely line A gift from you to me

IV

And all day long the day goes by Your line
echoes through my aching head today
(we'd drink to *wretched excess* so when
I heard the news I did again) Through wine
we tried to speak the truth each in his way
but you were better I held back and then
you chided me: 'Confess! Confess! All men
are sinners!' You loved high drama the play
of tragic forces you claimed had passed you by

This was never true Your life went the way
you aimed it: nowhere slowly Now mine
seems coarser I confess   *I confess!* In the sky
a plump mourning dove hoots its baleful cry
useless perhaps and yet how free   how fine

Fraxinus Nigra

And out of the earth made the Lord God to
grow every tree that is pleasant to the sight

Genesis 2:9

Father taught us the Latin names of trees

and we remember: *Quercus alba Ulmus*
americana though we rolled our eyes
at his recitals   Best of all we loved
the black ash in summer: we'd sprawl below
its oval canopy in the cool shade
or shoot out over the pond on the swing
he made   The smooth gray bark left powder
on our fingers   Father said Indians
made baskets from its wood

Now in the drift

of December when its leaves are gone
I stare at this stern skeleton
of tree against snow   Only in silhouette
can you see its symmetry the pattern
and structure of a long life its trunk
dividing high in a giant V the large
and smaller branches arching upward

the sturdy twigs like crosses against the sky

Birchbark

Because I'm used to a brick wall

and the asphalt street where surly gangs
will tip your garbage looking you in the eye
this view of trees and mountains seems unreal
stage props on celluloid   Back home
the old woman behind us was clubbed
to death in her bathtub the look
on her toothless face showing she had time
to think   They were after her TV: she almost
memorized the Rockford Files

                           Here the knuckled
branches scratch my window like extraterrestrial
fingers ground sloping away the slender
birches a see-through screen
to the distant hills the soundtrack
playing Prelude and Fugue no. 9
by Johann Sebastian Bach   What is life?
sings the tiny warbler so close I can see
the pale inside of her mouth   What is life?
sings the old lady in her bathtub The heart–
shaped leaves vibrate in and out of focus
I can count the veins   The warty stems
are reddish-brown with yellow spots   Below
this tracery of leaves the white bark curls
leaving black patches

                         I remember
from movies the Indian canoes
slashing through fast water with the ease
of total confidence in the natural world
while the birds fly low by my window

like captions in a foreign language

The Last Mountain Lion on Maple Crest Mountain

as told in the barbershop

Out there where Barnum Road hooks left
and disappears in the scrub
I was just out for turkey
doing my turkey call CHIK CHIK CHIK
worryin about all the rain
and how my potatoes was drownin like pups
and there he was not yellow
like you see on the goddam television
but graylike slick as a button
and lookin at me hard   No:
no way he was just some overgrown bobcat
that sucker was big as that table of yourn
with a tail this long Why ain't you heard
this before?   Because nobody
never told nobody nothin that's why
I weren't drinkin neither don't even
like the smell since I gave the stuff up
after me and Bob Willis shot
Pop Korsky's truck two years ago
I been livin here twenty years
and ain't never seen even an otter before
and Bob Willis has caught three can you believe
that bastard but it's been worth the wait:
I think someone wanted me to see that sonofabitch
before they drug my old bones away
and that's God's own unvarnished truth

Lines for the Reviewer

And if the critic is right
and those poems of no more worth
than a broken bottle scattered against the curb
or a dead bird in September's early bite
or the curse of a fetish priest in the modern world . . .

then there's nothing to do but hope
that the glass be sealed in cement in some way useful
that flowers spring from those weightless hollow bones
that the curse turn into a song to make children smile . . .

but if the critic is wrong
may he shred his fingers clambering over a wall
may he eat crow feet beak and feather
may his belly swell and his genitals wither . . .

Caitlin Rampant on a Field in Tuscany

In the southwest corner
of a field outside Castellina-in-Chianti
Caitlin is running through goldenrod
up to her chin   She has just learned to run
Stiff-kneed she gallops straight ahead
bent slightly forward somehow
as if enchanted not falling down   paying
no heed to our cries   Her shadow flutters
like a page two steps away

The March wind
rolls the buttery petals in waves
over the field and low overhead
small clouds squire the crows
Her scarf unfurls behind her like a banner
Olive trees shimmer (chalices cast
in a spell) the mountain purple
with distant music

Now the field
closes around her and she goes under
forging a trail only knights and magicians
can see charging against our wishes
toward the edge of the world unarmed
unshielded the old story: left
to her own device and ready for glory

One Hundred Robins

We had been freezing in separate wings

when the robins came puffed up and proud
ridiculous as senators round bellies
bobbing the branches acorns rattling the roof
like proclamations
                  Drunk on holly berries
they purpled our porch and picnic table
filibustering through the unraked leaves
chasing the sparrows like pages down the aisle

I thought I saw one smile
You thought you heard one burp
The sky swelled with its loosening rain

making amendments

The Shells of Bermuda

First the wind through the window lifting
this room with breath tugging the curtains waking
the flowers turning one by one slowly
the pages of old books   Then the sun
through the windows glinting in corners
warming the tops of tables   The cicadas'
shrill vibrations the woodpecker's percussion
even the high whine of Mrs Reinhold
as she scolds her children: 'Pamela!   Paul!'
All necessary but the window most of all

There are moments in every day
when a hunger seizes and the hands
tremble and a wall turns transparent
or a cup speaks   Suddenly
bright as the shells of Bermuda
the combs for your long hair blaze on the desk

Acknowledgments

Grateful acknowledgment is made to the following publications, in which some of these poems first appeared: *Appalachee Review* ("Caterpillar Plague, 2000"); *Arizona Quarterly* ("The Skiers," under the title "Cycle"); *Cantilevers* ("Epithalamion for Two Scientists"); *Christian Century* ("The Spindled World"); *Clockwatch* ("The True UFO Story"); *Cosmopolitan* ("Lilacs"); *Educational Forum* ("The Simplest Animals"); *5 AM* ("On Teaching Our Son to Tell Time," "M. Hoffstetler's Last Class"); *Formalist* ("Butterfly Cage," "Mystery"); *Green Mountains Review* ("American Youth," "Inheritance"); *Haerter* ("The Purity of Absolute Perfection," "Rocking Horse Winner"); *Isis* ("Blackberry Jam"); *Margie: The American Journal for Poetry* ("Brief Meditations on a Woodcut by Leonard Baskin," "The Death of Friends," "The Deserted Village, 2002," "The Pincushion," "P-town, '04"); *motive* ("What Wild-Eyed Murderer"); *Northwest Florida Review* ("The Little Factory, 1863," "Treasure Island"); *Poetry* ("Marine Forecast"); *Runes* ("Elderly, She Paints Another Nude"); *Southern Review* ("The Chemical Chain"); *Tampa Review* ("The Bookshelf," "The Contracted World," "The Director," "Fish Tale," "91st Birthday," "Turkish Coffee").

"Treasure Island" was commissioned by the *St. Petersburg Times* for their 2002 Christmas issue.

"Maples and Orange Trees, 2003" was commissioned by the City of St. Petersburg, Florida, for the twin birthdays of the two St. Petersburgs (Russia's 300th, Florida's 100th).

The Rat Poems was published as a chapbook by Bits Press, Cleveland, OH, in 1976.

Thanks to Converse College for appointing me Writer-in-Residence in 2002, and to the Fine Arts Work Center in Provincetown for residencies in 2003 and 2004, when some of these poems were written.

And thanks also to Arthur Skinner of Eckerd College for making the slide for the cover; and to P. C. Hodgell for allowing us to use her father's artwork.